Scribbling

on

JIVA, SHAVA & SHIVA

-Resonance of reality

Scribbling

on

JIVA, SHAVA & SHIVA

Author name: estranged master

Published by: Self-Published

ISBN: 978-93-5406-399-2

First published: 2020

Edited and typeset by Office of estranged master

Cover design by Neeraja Karthik

Contact e-mail Id: estrangedmaster@gmail.com

Chapters

In search of reality....1

Clarity in confusion 4

Transcending Sensibility makes a lot of Sense 18

Free-will vs. Destiny, karma & sublimation....30

Two Dolls from Same Clay 41

Ideal Vs. practical -WAY OF LIVING 57

Understand and unveil SHIVA....66

In search of reality

It's all the same and shall remain as such. The notion of this scribbling is to illuminate a thought to enquire about our mere existence.

The idea of this scribbling can be completed in a couple of pages but I have decided to make this complex abstract as plain as possible.

In this Scribbling, *I* and *My* denotes estranged master. *You* and *your* denotes reader and wherever **estranged master** is mentioned, it denotes the originator of thought in him.

Before understanding the concept of **GOD**, it is necessary to know why we need to understand this 'GOD', the abstract and unquantifiable experience. In the same way, we lead a life without knowing 'what is life'. We project our ideas about life as a definition to it but we don't know 'life'.

What is the purpose of living and how to identify the origin of it? - This scribbling tries to explore the same.

Let there be different paths, let there be different ideas, let there be contrasts, let there be consensuses but there shall be only one truth for all, irrespective of land and time.

This scribbling does not try to prove, conceptualize the abstract or personify Shiva. It merely tries to provoke the enquiry into reality and to see Shiva as an essence by nature.

This Scribbling mentions the terms like Jiva, Shava, Jada, Consciousness, Mind, dharma Atman, and way of living, the purpose of living, free-will, and destiny and so on. All these terms bring out a different notion altogether.

Beliefs are different from reality. What we think as real will fade out when we realize the reality.

What we think as real might turn into an illusion. The belief in rationality might become questionable. Everything under this gamut can be disputed. Every life has its views which fails against the time. Ideas are different from existence and Shiva is more than the concept of 'GOD'

This scribbling tries to invoke the thought in you. Rather than seeing this scribbling as a book, try to experience it. What is irrational today might be rational tomorrow.

Everything is knowledge until you are not bound by it.

Everything is real until you realize it.

And when you realize it

I AM YOU

-estranged master

Clarity in confusion

The response from Mr. Ananda, so-called spiritually awakened person to the question –'Who are you?' would be 'I am Atman'.

Whereas estranged master asks 'Are you not Jiva who is bound to become Shava (corpse) and a Jada (inert) as time passes?'

Then estranged master gets a reply from Mr. Ananda that 'Body shall die but atman, the reality of Atman shall not die and shall not be bound by cycle of time.'

Confused estranged master asks 'I understood that concept of atman cannot be comprehended by our senses but my question is 'are you a living entity or non-living – Jiva or Shava?'

Mr. Ananda says 'Since I am replying to you, can you consider me as a living entity?'

Estranged master asks 'you are replying since your intent says so. Suppose if your intent says not to reply, can you be considered as non -living?'

Mr. Ananda replies 'Since I am Jiva, my intent says me to reply or at least react. I breathe, I walk, and I stand in front of you to answer your silly question. This conclusively proves that I am living. I am embodied with life forces. I am not inert and what more do you need me to prove?'

Estranged Master says 'I agree to what you said but how can you conclusively say that only **you** are acting with **your** intent and not someone else making you act, maybe the originator of your intent?'

Mr. Ananda replies 'To tell precisely, you can see that I speak, walk and act. This should satisfy you that I am living.'

Estranged Master says 'I agree to what you said but I don't believe in input from my senses completely. The reason is; prior apprehensions and knowledge with my experiences can give a different perception altogether.'

Mr. Ananda asks 'What is your point on this worthless argument?'

Estranged Master says 'I am wondering that how to define that I am a Jiva?'

Mr. Ananda says 'It is simple. The moment when you are born you are Jiva and the moment your prana leaves, you become Shava.'

Estranged master says 'In simple, Jiva is the embodiment with prana.'

Mr. Ananda elatedly replies 'Yes. See you were not able to understand this simple concept.'

Estranged master says 'I already knew this because I am born and I am bound to die. I am constricted to space, time and matter but who is the originator of my thought to confirm that **I am Jiva**?'

Mr. Ananda says 'There is no originator. You are the origin of your thoughts.'

Estranged Master 'This is my inconclusive doubt. The thought of **MY** and **I** appear at the instance of my birth and disappears or becomes unidentifiable when I am dead. Does that mean Atman which is claimed to be unborn, claimed to transcend space and time is indifferent from Jiva? It is imperative to identify my existence with my actions and thoughts which are bound by time and matter but this cannot conclusively define my existence.'

Mr. Ananda 'You are too confusing.'

Estranged Master 'At least I have clarity in my confusion.'

After this conversation, **estranged Master self-enquires:**

What is the origin of my fear, sadness, happiness, hatred, and love? Is it based on input I derive? Is it based on the impact of my past experiences? Is it my knowledge and my intelligence that determines how I live, what I am or what I shall become?

When such questions arose in my mind then it's time to analyse those thoughts. But why I need to think about all these? It does not change my birth and death. The transition from Jiva to Shava is inevitable. Rather than thinking and self-analysing, why can't I enjoy every minute of my life. Even if I question and self- analyse the purpose of living, my day –to –day living becomes questionable and agitated.

On average, I would hardly live for 36000 days. Out of which at least one-third of my life would go in *sleep* where **I** don't do anything except ignoring **MY** life which can be considered as *bliss* for a limited time.

Whether **I am** in the path of self-realisation or enjoying every material aspect shall not stop me from becoming Shava at some point in time.

The purpose of devotion on GOD and knowledge on self might be futile because a person who is self-realized and a person who enjoys everything around him in a materialistic way are going to face the same destiny. The concept of the ***afterlife*** might not even exist. It might be a hallucination or fantasy of our ancestors. The only existence is now.

Why complicate things which cannot be explained and not sure whether it exists?

Why do we need to know the origin or originator of us?

What is the reason to know who am I? There are thousands of scriptures across generations which explains the purpose of self-realisation i.e. liberation; where liberation is subjected to many interpretations depending upon different schools of philosophy. It conclusively tells that idea of liberation is not the truth but mere perception.

The realisation might even stop at a point where the person may not be able to transcend beyond; with an assumption that he has realized. It entirely depends on individual perception. In the state of Jiva, at least the source of happiness can be ascertained, explained and experienced. It can be easily be inferred that life ends with death like every creature on this earth. Though the concept of reincarnation has been *explained by many*, the concept of karma and the *afterlife* maybe only the ideas that are posed as truth. Why we need to *waste* time, knowing the fact that it is limited. I am not religious as I don't worship ***unless I feel it is worthy of my worship***. I may be spiritual but I am not sure, as the concept of spirituality and religion overlaps each other and often gets confused. What if my life ends with death and has to re-begin again?

Estranged master is bored, tired, agitated but still confused. When questions were projected to Mr. Ananda; estranged master had a sense of satisfaction that he had required intelligence to question Mr. Ananda and make him falter. Estranged master's ego was satisfied.

But when questions were self –imposed, estranged master's intelligence and ego makes no sense as he is **in search of truth** and recognizing his ego and showcasing his intelligence upon himself was absurd and senseless. Estranged master perception entirely changed on the concept of reasoning.

Within a glimpse of an eye, estranged master realised that there may be **certain aspects which cannot be explained but can only be experienced and since it has not been experienced, its existence cannot be denied.**

If such experiences were tried to be explained, it can only be perceptions and ideas on experiences and not the **absolute truth**. Even the gross experiences from sensory pleasures cannot be explained as such an explanation on experiences differ from person to person.

Moreover, my queries and confusion were about the ways to know what am I. These queries shall apply to Mr. Ananda, myself and every human around. However, the key to prove the origin of my existence is not by enquiring about others. When I want to find what I am, the only source of knowledge to know about me is 'I". This is when I have to enquire I, whereas the state of 'My' has to be stripped down to 'I' i.e. MY attributes, behavior, intelligence, and ego cannot really reveal WHAT I AM.

To complicate further within a short period, estranged master understood that 'I question I about I' and 'I have to answer about I to I. Does it apply to estranged master alone or these questions apply to ***everyone***?

The path of self-enquiry shall apply to any being on this earth born with the mind. If the process of self–enquiry is same for every human, the realisation of truth behind such self–enquiry should also be the same. Then knowing about *Self* means knowing about everyone and everything around. Which cannot be seen but can only be experienced or just exist in and out there. '**This is the reality of realisation**'.

But how this perception can be justified? What are the chances of having different answers from different persons on self –enquiry? What are the chances of multiple realities?

REMEMBER; if there are multiple realities then it is not **real**. How can there be Different truths?? There can be different ways to experience the truth but there can be only one truth which is constant and absolute. If the truth is challenged, it means an idea has been posed as truth.

Source of knowledge like scriptures can be considered as a compilation of experiences on absolute truth. It can be neither be negated nor gives us the answer to self-enquiry. It gives an idea on reality but the realisation of reality can reveal only when a person '*starts searching within.*'

Without alphabets, I cannot form letters and without letters, I cannot write sentences. Scriptures such as

Upanishads are alphabets for the **self-enquiry**. It connotes the experiences on absolute truth by realized.

A tricky question: Since *Upanishads* can be considered as an *explanation* of only experiences on truth, can Upanishads be challenged?

Answering YES would be absurd because unless I know the *truth*, I cannot challenge any other experience on truth and when I start searching within, it serves no purpose in challenging such explanations as these are individual experiences. What does this '**start searching within**' mean? Let us understand this from the 'self' perspective.

When I am the absolute and only source of knowledge to know the truth about 'I' which is also the truth about everything, I am everything.

When I know I am everything, I have nothing to give and take. The giving, taking, enjoying, satisfaction, ego, intelligence, knowledge, etc.; makes no sense, as the truth of 'I' is beyond emotions and inflictions. Trying to know about self through senses would be absurd since there is no way to know about 'I' from others and other sources i.e. external factors.

I am not what I think, I am not what I do, I am not what I feel, I am not what I see, I am not what I sense, I cannot define me based on gender, living, ability as all these attributes wade of by time but the reality of 'I' standstill there as such transcending space and time.

Like the same person who is a father to his daughter, son to his mother and husband to his wife; attitude, perceptions, behavior, the way we think, the way we speak, the way we act and react changes depending upon the time, place and people around.

But what does not change? With or without the awareness, the reality of 'I' does not change.

The reality of 'I' can be called as **Brahman** or P**aramatma, Mahavishnu, Eswara** or in an infinite number of ways but it cannot be identified with an attribute. Senses clog reality by making the mind to believe that I am dependent on external factors to understand what I am. It becomes like a cloud of dust on a window which hinders the capability to radiate light.

As a creature with a mind, I have to live on my senses. These inputs with an application of cognitive ability makes me to differentiate between good, bad, lie, truth and results me with pain and pleasure.

Trying to experience and realise 'I' with external factors makes no sense. When the reality of 'I' is beyond the comprehension of senses, trying to realize it with the help of the same senses is absolute nonsense.

And ……………..

Transcending Sensibility makes a lot of Sense

Who am I and what am I doing here?

This can be considered as an intrinsic question that comes into the mind of every individual as the first step towards self –enquiry. To be precise, the path of self - enquiry can confuse, make you adore, oblige and acknowledge reality without making any 'Sense'. However, with inference and conviction, the realisation of reality reveals the veil between real and unreal. When a person is born, his 'lifetime' shall be predominantly based on inputs from sensory, filtering through senses and recording such inputs in the brain with all apprehensions, permutations & combination including the application of intelligence rendered by un-identifiable abstract called "mind'.

In simple, this is life. Though we live based on inputs we derive from our sensory organs, the origin of our thoughts and awareness on existence cannot be exactly determined.

If we give a 'thought'; the origin of our intellect, thoughts, apprehension which appears with birth, stays with us based on the need and disappears when the Jiva becomes 'Shava'.Where does this awareness veil when Jiva becomes Shava?

In reality, the awareness of 'I' and 'my' can determine why we live and how we live but awareness of 'My' constantly changes based on need and situation. Whereas, the awareness of 'I' is constant and indifferent from our existence until Jiva transcends Shava.

Does is it mean that 'can the origin of I be the root cause of our existence'?

If awareness of 'I' is the original state of existence, how to explain, experience and conceptualize this abstract?

First of all, let us differentiate between Sensory, Sense, and Sensibility. For example, a fan in your house makes a subtle noise continuously. Though you hear it, sense it, your mind chooses to ignore it. To make it simple, your sensory organs receive it but you are involuntarily trained to ignore it. In the same way, sensory organs throw continuous and random inputs from around but you sense or ignore it based on need and awareness. Sensing is an ability to perceive data and filter inputs for your knowledge or intelligence to emote further. However such sensing gives sensibility coupled with knowledge as a complementing attribute to your existence but cannot define the original state of existence i.e. 'I'. Your mind does all the functions to train your senses for sensibility which is necessary for your survival. However, too much emphasis on senses makes us only sensible but ignores the original state – experiencing the reality of 'I'.

If someone questions your awareness, your straight thought would be about your awareness with external factors. This is mere sensibility, a resulting action to your inference from senses. However, this cannot define your existence.

By virtue, awareness has always been considered as responsiveness projected outwards in reaction to inference through senses. As said before, this state of awareness is not perpetual. However, the awareness of 'I' remains constant and undeterred which is perpetual and not dependent on your Sensory, Senses or Sensibility. Experiencing the reality of 'I' reveals the greatest mystery - What am I? But real 'I' gets impaired by completely depending on inference from senses for understanding it. We fail to realize and experience what we are since 'I' gets subdued by 'MY'.

What does this really mean?

Classification or identification through 'my' is not real. Explanation of myself is not real. ***Only experiencing 'I' is real.***

We need to realize and understand that the Mind which creates the rudimentary state of consciousness also makes us think that it is indifferent from our body and emotions.

When a question arises - how are you bound with this earth and what binds you with this earthly matter? None can give a definitive answer.

When someone questions himself that why is he here in this world? And what is he doing here? It stirs up the whole purpose of living.

Being senseless is absolute bliss but once you start living, 'external factors' encompass your mind and do not allow you to traverse in the path of self–enquiry.

We have to accept that:

Reality of self, name it God, Brahman, supersensuous or absolute truth is beyond our comprehension. This cannot be understood or realized with the help of Senses.

If such reality can be perceived with the help of senses then reality should be a day-to-day experience but still, the origin of Jiva remains as the biggest mystery. This indicates that the answer to the origin of 'I' is supersensuous.

If someone says 'My Senses perceive everything around me and maybe I failed to recognize and realize the reality around' then estranged master interprets this differently.

1. In a simple sense, the world is not an illusion because whatever you perceive from it with your inference

makes your experience as 'real' but this becomes an illusion only when you realise the reality.

2. If we do a classic comparison: awake vs. Dream; in the state of dream, everything would be experienced as real until you wake up. Supposedly if you are hurt and bleeding in the dream, when you wake up such experience disappears. Whereas if you are hurt and bleeding when you are awake such experience shall be real in nature and does not disappear until you disappear.

3. Even if you get killed in a dream, it becomes an illusion once you wake up but till you wake up, your dream shall be your reality.

4. What we perceive around us shall not stay there as it is because of constant changing and such a state cannot be an attribute to reality.

5. For example, there are *n* number of people and these people do not perceive, understand the world in the same way as people do have their own understanding on this world and life. If the world we perceive is not constant and not the same for every person, it is not the reality. **'It is our wisdom to understand that there are no multiple Truths.'** As said before, there can be only different perceptions on Truth.

6. When we overindulge on our senses, we fail to differentiate between reality and perception. Moreover, there is a minuscule difference between perceptions on truth and **experiencing the truth**. Perceptions are multiple sheaths that pose a comprehensive idea on truth whereas experiencing the truth is the reality behind all those ideas.

7. Sensory perceptions yield no result. When you blink, the world tends to disappear but it remains there because you know so; it is your knowledge.

8. But where does this world go while you are in deep sleep? You tend to sleep in a belief that when you wake up, your world stays the same but awareness of your existence in deep sleep is always questionable since you are not able to perceive this altered state of existence with your senses and intelligence.

9. You are still Jiva in deep sleep but you don't realize it. Is it because your mind also sleeps or is it because your mind is not able to comprehend this state without any inputs?

10. We can conclude that while dreaming, your mind works but your senses do not. For instance, how a dream is created without any inputs? In a state of dream, how do you see without using your eyes, how do you hear

without using your ears? To simplify further, your mind creates a dream with inputs from your mind which shall be experienced by your mind. Your concept of senses becomes absurd in your dream as you create your own world without any external factors.

11. With the above said, it can be concluded that your mind has the power to imagine, understand, experience things without any inputs. However, your mind is trained to grasp and infer only from sensory inputs. For instance, the more you practice something, you tend to do it without focal awareness; call it subconscious, memory, intelligence or training. Mind answers based on past experiences and inputs from the present. It exhibits the required intelligence for further understanding and decisions.

12. The mind is also trained to imagine; as imagination becomes a major aspect of our decision making and foreseeing.

13. The mind is also trained to distract and concentrate based on need, pleasure, and satisfaction and to forget pain, inflictions in some instances.

14. But we forgot a major aspect: Mind is never trained to be still. Neither calm nor silent. **TO BE STILL**

15. But what train's this Mind or who train this Mind. Is there something beyond Mind which instructs it to act accordingly?

16. This state of stillness reveals 'I'. In deep sleep, our mind is STILL but it happens as an accident. This makes us fail in comprehending this altered state of existence.

17. Does this mean that the identity of 'I' self-reveals only in deep sleep? The answer is NO. The basic tenet of deep sleep is the stillness of mind. However, you don't realize it since your mind fails to comprehend it. If your

mind is trained to understand and experience stillness, it reveals and makes us realize this abstract within a fraction of a second. When awake, one cannot shut down the senses but when the stillness of mind is achieved, he can voluntarily ignore his senses. State of mind defines your life and purpose to your actions but the stillness of mind defines everything. ***True self shall reveal only when you become 'Senseless'.***

18. If someone lives in hallucination, we call him lunatic, insane and different other names. We judge him based on his behavior with family, society, compliance with societal norms and his belief in hallucinations. If experiencing reality makes you understand that the world is an illusion, all your beliefs about the world shall unveil as hallucination and your sensible life will become senseless.

If life has to transcend from sensible to senseless, how this sense gets wrecked by destiny and free-will?

This Jiva has multiple paths to lead a life. Though paths are different, it shall lead to the same destination. There are two things which can be considered as DESTINY. One is 'birth' and one is 'death'. Nobody can change these two. Nobody knows when he will be born unless he comes on to this earth and none can predict the exact time of their death. With the advancement of science and technology, humans think death can be deferred but it can neither be ignored nor avoided.

IF SOMEONE SAYS DESTINY CANNOT BE CHANGED – YES, IT CANNOT BE CHANGED. Destiny is same for any being on this earth i.e. birth and the death and what happens between birth and death is not same for every human being

Transition from Jiva to Shava is destined and the ability to decide i.e. Free-will defines the way of living and purpose of living. Free will defines the ability to 'create and choose life'. I am not talking about success and achievement here. No one can universally define success and achievement. The idea of success and achievement is different for every individual.

In a simple sense, GOD has given us free hand to 'play with our own life'. Let me tell you a short story about an experience: I was on my way to Neelkanth Mahadev Temple near Rishikesh. As usual, I started to walk up the hill without a sweater. The weather was cold enough for a need of thermal wear. To my surprise – a sudden Hailstorm. At that moment, I realized a need for a sweater. I started to shiver with a feeling that I might end up in a state of hypothermia.

I rushed into a tea stall and ordered hot tea. There sat a man who was chewing tobacco and enjoying the hailstorm. In the tea stall, a couple was standing next to me. This person who was chewing tobacco, told me to sit next to him. He asked me: Do you know the difference between 'I LOVE YOU and YOU ARE MY LOVE'. I had no clue. He said that 'I LOVE YOU' ends up in dissolution, whereas 'YOU ARE MY LOVE' ends up in realisation. I said I did not understand.

He said: There was person named Chidananda. During his adulthood, he went to a woman and said 'I LOVE YOU' they ended up marrying and had kids. Chidananda loved his kids. His wife and his kids loved him. Chidananda loved his parents.

He loved his siblings. He loved everything. Everyone loved Chidananda. He was considered to be a personification of pure love and he was spiritual too. Chidananda LOVED GOD THE MOST. As time started to fly, by virtue of death, people loved by Chidananda started to disappear. Chidananda got dejected, depressed and was left in agony. At some juncture, Chidananda disappeared from the people he loved. He reached GOD's place and determined to question GOD.

When Chidananda saw GOD, he questioned: Why people around me disappeared and when I died, I had to leave everyone around me in agony and make them suffer in pain? Why did you make me suffer and others suffer because of my death? I loved you the most but still, you betrayed me.

GOD: Did I tell you to love me?

Chidananda: No but I considered you as my friend, guide and as a source to lead me in a good way. I loved you unconditionally.

GOD: If you have loved me unconditionally then how can you say that I betrayed you and why did you expect me to be your friend and guide. When you expect something from me, it is not unconditional.

Chidananda: I was devoted upon you, adored you, worshipped you but you did not even consider me.

GOD: Who asked you to worship me?

Chidananda: So you did not love me? When you can't even reciprocate love, you are not even worthy of worship.

GOD: ***I won't love you and I won't bless you*** **because** ***you are the manifestation of my Love***. I created everything for you. I created obstacles, illusions. I gave you discriminatory knowledge. I did also this for you without expecting anything from you.

Chidananda: Then why did you create us?

GOD: When you believe that you are created then I become the creator. When you believe that you are not created then I become an observer. When you believe that you are the creator, I imbibe. I am not bound by time and space. I wanted to experience myself when I am bound by space and time. Then ***I became you. I even gave myself so many obstacles as an illusion and free-will as light in the darkness. But I started to search in darkness with darkness. This is when I became a mere creator of you as ignorance created wrongful discrimination***

There ends the story and hailstorm.

Free-will is the only attribute that differentiates humans from other beings on this Earth. To us, this characteristic is to such an extent that we can even decide whether to live or die.

As said before, though this transition may be illusory, unless you realize it, the transition shall be real. Between this Jiva and Shava, you shall be imposed with many obstacles as questions to your life.

Everyone has some kind of understanding on the term 'achievement'. When we try to strive towards it, such striving may not result as expected. This applied ability i.e. free –will even make you conquer so-called failure. You term and name a shortfall of achievement as failure only when you succumb to it.

When you gracefully accept to choose a different path altogether or to strive again in the same path such decisions shall become your answer for short-fall. Life puts out multiple questions in front of us and we tend to reply to everything till we reach our destiny. Every reply might not turn out as expected by us. We have the greatest gift to gracefully accept the defeat and move on or we can attempt the same question without accepting our defeat. At the end of the tunnel, everything fades away. This free-will can be called as ability, content, intelligence, understanding, and judgment and so on but really what does this ability mean to us?

When coursed in right sense, it gives us the meaning of life. Though Moon tells us that night has arrived and Sun tells the day, we should not forget that Moon shines because of Sun, as Moon does not illuminate on its own. In the same way, your intelligence can only defer but cannot deny destiny. The free-will cannot question destiny and it is always under the realm of it, like a Moon which cannot avoid Sun. ***Life is seriously not serious.***

Enjoy everything in life with a small remembrance to accept in a way it is delivered and striving does not satiate. Life is like a big circus, shows you everything. You tend to see a circus, play daily. After some time, you tend to get bored with what is available in a circus. You expect more from it. This is when the problem arises, desires become need. There are things which you have consumed so much to say that it is enough for life but you will still crave for it again after some time. This is when you get succumbed to your desires.

Until you unveil Shiva, your understanding on desires decides your way of living. *When someone says liberation is a desire, to be happy is a desire, to have peace of mind is also a desire; my reply would be: liberation, to be happy and peace are only different states of mind?* When you desire something, the next question would be: what do you need to fulfill the desire. When you see happiness as your ultimate desire, you need certain factors; be it people, things or situations to make you happy. It means you are completely dependent on certain factors to be happy. When you want something and you don't get it, your desire becomes desperation, the more desperation you have, the more desecration it does.

Inability to achieve the sense of satisfaction creates hatred and the whole purpose of desire gets lost. Though no one can shun down desires immediately, sublimating it shows you a practical way. Don't crave for it, receive it without any hindrance.

Happiness lies in subtlest things, realize it & relish it. Rather than craving for something, minimize your cravings. Ego and Pride are created by your mind. The same Mind can also create bliss without external factors. Your Mind has the ability (free-will) to even perceive bliss without depending on anything. It starts where it stops; Senselessness. Limiting is not sublimating. What is this 'Sublimating'? Understand the difference between need and desire. Remember whatever you enjoy does not stay as such. Rather than such enjoyment deserting you, keep a tab on such enjoyment. Human lives run on desires but when such desires become an obsession, you get succumbed to it. *Practically, accept a sense of enjoyment that sustains with you for a long time.* In reality, the susceptibility of the mind cannot differentiate between need and greed. There is nothing easier than experiencing happiness without depending on external factors for such happiness. If someone asks 'Do you want to be happy?' The understood one shall answer, 'I am happiness' when someone asks how you can be so happy. Understood one says: How can you quantify and qualify the term happiness? As I am experiencing it without expressing and when someone asks: What makes you happy? Understood one will say: Nothing except understanding the reality of life.

If things go overboard:

Envy creates hatred, Desperation creates despair,

Inability creates anger and pride makes you falter.

In a simple sense, WHEN YOU CANT AVOID, LIMIT IT. According to estranged master, this is sublimating and this is the sensible way for happiness. ***Sublimating does not become a hindrance for experiencing your life to fullest because perception on the purpose of living, way of living do contrast from one person to another. However, when you***

'really' understand what is needed and what is not, all the Contrast shall become Consensus.

Two Dolls from Same Clay

Once upon a time, a king thought of going to all the religious places in and around his kingdom. During his journey, he saw a sage at a foothill. The sage was just laughing to himself with closed eyes. The king thought that sage must be a lunatic. While returning, the king saw the same sage sleeping and giggling in repeat. The king thought sage must be having some dreams in which he is fulfilling his fantasies. The king also thought that if he has so much of desire rather than being a sage, he can lead a normal life where he can 'enjoy' his life.

The king decides to rest for some time and camped overnight. The next day he saw sage crossing over his camp.

The King called sage and asked 'I was watching you for a couple of days. First time when I saw, you were laughing to yourself with closed eyes and talking to yourself. The second time when I saw, you were sleeping with a smiling face and giggling. I understand that you have desires. Since you do not have power, money or anything, I will help to fulfill your desire.'

Sage replied 'If you are ready to help, I am good with wine and women. I am also ready to accept any other gifts like gold, money or a position in your ministry.'

King: 'When you have so much of greed, why did you become a sage? You can lead a **normal way of life** like others where you can work, earn money, drink wine, marry and have kids.'

Sage: 'What is a **normal way of life?'**

King: 'Happy life which you intended to live.'

Sage: 'Can you define **happy life?'**

King: 'Sufficient money which can be earned for living and bestow some property to my sons and daughters.'

Sage: 'If this is how you define a happy life then except you no one in your kingdom is leading a happy life.'

King got surprised and asked 'How can you say that? My kingdom is the richest. I have provided my people with security, a proper society, moral values and good resources for living.'

Sage: 'My dear King, nobody has money to spend on what they desire. Nobody can define *sufficiency*. People feel that they have very little money to inherit to their sons and daughters because the money they earn on day to day basis won't be even sufficient and satisfying their basic needs. As per your definition, except for a few, no one is leading a happy life.

King got astonished and did not know how to reply.

King: 'I will think and try to define a happy life.'

Sage: 'You have to define two things. What is the happiest way of living and the purpose of such living?'

The sage goes back and waits for a call. The king called sage after a week. In that one week, the king along with his council of ministers tried to define 'what is the happiest way of living and purpose of such living'. After a week, sage comes to the king's camp with two puppies in his hand. While the king was trying to explain the happiest way of living, sage leaves puppies on the floor.

King surprisingly asked why sage left puppies on the floor. Sage calmly answers that 'Earth also belongs to these puppies.'

King gets irritated and says that 'How can you say so? I am the king of this kingdom, I conquered this land to rule over my people with integrity and I am not bound to anyone in this land except my conscience.

But sage politely answers: 'But you are bound by the eternal law. The truth which transcends any kingdom. I name it Dharma. You name it differently but you cannot deny it. We have to accept that we carry different views on life but the life we experience is neither illusion nor real but a veil to make us understand that you and I are the same.'

King gets shocked and says: 'I do believe in God. I do believe in Vedas and your reply does not even make any sense to me.'

Sage: 'As definite as death follows birth and birth follows death, happiness follows after understanding and accepting the true purpose of living. When you are not even able to explain the purpose of living, what is the purpose of living then?

King gets riddled and puzzled. His whole perception of visiting temples and pilgrimages get destroyed in seconds.

Sage explains to king calmly: 'though you say that you study Vedas, visit temples, your greed and ego i.e. altered state of your pride makes you think that you are invincible.'

King: 'I am invincible now.'

Sage: 'I agree with that. You have the power to behead me right now. I die at this moment but you will follow me in some matter of time. You are killing me only to satisfy your anger and ego. In this process, you are also killing your happiness and peace. You may subdue your agitation and feel that killing me would provide you a sense of peace but your guilt cannot be avoided.'

King understands clearly that there is no definitive way for determining the happiest way of living but there are ways which will lead you to unhappiness. Actions with intent to hurt others and injuring self with the ego that falters at some point in time.

King: 'The answer for the happiest way of living is simple i.e. not to injure others intentionally because it injures one's happiness and peace.'

Sage: 'Yes. Shall we go and meet your people in disguise.'

King readily accepts and goes to his kingdom in a disguised manner, like a beggar along with sage. Few people shouted at them. Few people rendered them alms.

The king is surprised that though economic status is almost equal in all houses, only a few people have rendered alms and not everyone.

King got into confusion and asked sage that why only a few people rendered him alms?

The king: 'According to you, many families are not even meeting their basic needs but how few families refused while others rendered.'

Sage: 'If actions are not coupled with greed, ego, and unnecessary desired results, everybody in your kingdom would have given alms. Desire does not change your existence but people relate ego and pleasure received through senses as the real meaning of existence. Like ego is always a false replication of existence, anger an altered state of inability, pride is a misunderstood way to validate the quality of living. This is a basic human tendency. This cannot be changed. This is always based on individual perceptions. If you rule this kingdom for sovereignty, you would always want your son or daughter to be your heir without considering their ability to rule and perform their duty as a king but if you rule to only safeguard your people and resources which creates a peaceful kingdom then you would accept a better capable person as your successor to your throne. Though you know your children might not be as capable as you, still you will make him or her as your successor. This is how human tendencies work.'

King: 'How in some houses they rendered alms?'

Sage: 'There are two things; when they have more than what they need (again this is based on individual perceptions to define NEED) or when they like to spread and share happiness. As I said to you before, if you are trying to kill me, it is as good as killing your happiness and peace. Happiness is infectious but the effects of it make things better. As I told before, human tendencies won't change. However consciously avoiding to injure someone physically, verbally, mentally and injuring one-self with pride, the ego is more than suffice.'

King: 'I agree to it. If I apply your principle as a king, I need to kill my enemies in war. As defined by you, even killing my enemies would kill my happiness and peace. I will never be happy and will always be filled with selfishness and greed. How do you define it and put me out of this puzzle.'

Sage smiled and said: 'As I said before intent matters.'

King: 'I need to kill someone to save my throne. The reason for such an act can be seen as an act of selfishness and greed but it makes me happy as I am saving my throne.'

Sage: 'If you fight your enemies thinking as a duty to protect people of your kingdom, saving your throne becomes an ancillary outcome to your desired result. In this, you intend to save your people more than your throne. Whereas you kill a person only to save your throne, you have failed as a king since your duty to protect people gets maligned and overtaken by your greed. See your position as a duty rather than power.'

King: 'What if I am doing it as an act of self-defense.'

Sage: 'You are also part of this kingdom. Self-defense means defending and not killing. As I said, intent matters.'

King: 'Is it all enough to have a happy life?'

Sage laughed and said: 'In a real sense there is nothing called a happy life. Remember a week ago, you asked why I was laughing at myself and why I was smiling while sleeping. By virtue, happiness is a mere indicator of the quality of life. If happiness gets inflicted and affected by certain factors, you are not living your own life.'

King: 'what does that mean?'

Sage asks the king: 'what do you think about women and wine? What do you get out of both?'

King irrelevantly replies: 'One satisfies my thirst and one satisfies my lust.'

The sage abruptly stops and says: 'why water can't satisfy your thirst? Why wine? And how do you define satisfaction of lust? Wine is an altered state of an existing substance that is already there. If you can identify by what substance is wine made up of; then directly consume such fruits.

King says: 'It is not about the fruit or wine. It is about the experience felt by consuming wine.'

Sage: 'A human body is mere flesh and bones in a different form, be it for women or men. It is about how we see, what we think and what we perceive out of it.

The uniqueness of every identifiable individual's mind is the greatest attribute to human but when you try to put everything into the concept of sensory, the whole concept of mind makes no sense. As experiencing reality is more than explaining, your experience is more than input you get through sensory.'

King says: 'If wine and women are the external factors which give input through my sensory, such sense of experience makes me happy.'

Sage: Can you keep on drinking wine forever?

King: 'No there is a limit to it.'

Sage: 'Your experience on happiness or bliss is only for a limited time and such experience is completely dependent on external factors. It is a vicious cycle between need and a sense of satisfaction. Bliss stays with you till the time when you feel the need for it, there starts your desperation. What makes you happy?'

King: 'My power, my people, food I eat, the wine I drink and children around me who will become future leaders to lead a righteous life.'

Sage: 'Let's say if something goes wrong and assume you lose your throne, you don't have kids and there is a severe drought in your kingdom. In this situation, what will be your state of mind?'

King: 'I can endure any of these problems for some time after that I might get crumbled for the need of it.'

Sage: 'See, your experience of happiness is directly derived from the necessity of external factors. Whereas my happiness is not dependent on any external factors. My happiness is not even dependent on my senses.'

King: 'My way of experiencing happiness makes sense to me. Whereas, your way of experiencing happiness is senseless to me.'

Sage: 'My bliss is not dependent on anything. My bliss is eternal. This state can neither have an attribute nor defined. It is perpetual. My joy of living is not based on the purpose. My bliss is senseless & selfless. My bliss comes from sharing and caring without getting attached to it.

King gets shocked: 'Is it why you were giggling before. Does that stop you from dreaming on these things like material aspects?'

Sage says: 'If I dream about material aspects rather than dreaming about it, I shall crave to experience it. My source of happiness is in realizing the self, accepting the truth and understanding life. When I understood that such bliss is not dependent on anything, why I need happiness through my senses which can also make me sober?'

King: 'How do you make yourself happy?'

Sage: 'I am not creating happiness, I personify it. I share radiance of it till this Jiva transcends.' This is the ultimate truth. This is a fraction of path in knowing the self. As we discussed, the purpose of living is always based on individual perception but if we understand and accept a righteous way of living with content and sublimating then the purpose of living and happiness follows on.'

King: 'I understand. The right way of living makes oneself identify his purpose of living and such a sense of satisfaction creates happiness. A person can live by understanding that the whole conscience with less attachment like a water drop on a lotus leaf. Bliss comes when we begin to accept things around us that are temporary in nature including 'ME and MY'. The sense of detachment towards attachment makes happiness independent and the purpose of living can be considered as a duty than actions for the desired outcome.'

Ideal Vs. practical -WAY OF LIVING

Sage: 'If someone has taken up brahmacharya and lays down a self-imposed rule by which he prohibits himself from touching woman, he justifies his brahmacharya with righteousness. Here comes a situation, where he sees a woman drowning in a river. He goes and saves her though it violates his self-imposed rule. What kind of an act do you see in this? Was he right in saving a woman's life by dishonoring his brahmacharya or has he failed to lead an ideal way of living by violating self – imposed rule?'

King: 'Though his brahmacharya goes futile, saving a woman's life proves his righteousness. We can conclude that he sacrificed his ideology to save a woman's life.'

Sage: 'can we conclude that he weighed the value of life is more than his ideology? He saw the practicality of the situation rather than sticking to his ideology.

King replies: 'Yes. He understood the value of life.'

Sage says: 'In this scenario, it is about saving a life. In some other scenarios, you will be always be forced to choose between multiple decisions where every decision seems to be right. Your way of living is determined based on deciding between these decisions. The practical way of life is exhibited on a need basis. A temporary action for the sustenance of integrity and righteousness.'

King asks: 'But integrity and righteousness are subjective by nature?'

Sage replies: 'Everything is subjective except truth. As said before, the way of living defines our understanding of integrity and righteousness. Being ideal is not always practical and being practical is not always ideal but when you limit your aspirations towards personal favoured outcomes on your decisions, it is simple as encasing your mind from inflictions and affections.' To do a comparison, I am taking two manifestations for this; Shri Rama for the ideal way of life and Shri Krishna for a practical way of life. Both of them dealt with great difficulties in life. Both of them were righteous in their paths. Situations differed, actions varied, outcomes have been chaos but both upheld integrity to the duty assigned. In both manifestations, a sense of responsibility was more evident than the execution of authority.

Shri Rama was the personification of a man who led an ideal way of life. He was always righteous in his thoughts and actions. When people point out about Shri Rama left Sitha over the people of his kingdom, we should also acknowledge that Shri Rama left his kingship for 14 years to oblige his father's promise to his step-mother. A promise to which he was never involved with.

Shri Rama endured so many problems, sufferings, and dilemmas in his life but he stood with his duty and righteousness as a king.

Shri Rama could have said to his father that he is not obliged to bind by the promise made by his father to Kaikeyi but Shri Rama did not want his father to falter. He obliged his father's words. Can we call this as affection or can we consider his deed as son's duty towards father?

Let us take Shri Krishna on the other side. Shri Krishna was considered as God who walked on this Earth. He was able to perform miracles and outwit everyone around. Shri Krishna did everything even after understanding the repercussions of his actions. The reason was simple, for the sustenance of Dharma.

Shri Krishna considered all his actions and decisions as need of the hour without putting himself in dilemma. Though decisions did not benefit him in any way, he performed actions as duty without expecting any self-desired outcomes out of such action.

We need to realize that somewhere between Adharma and Dharma, there lies 'Apadharma.' What Shri Krishna did was Apadharma. The need of the hour. A balancing act to restore the Dharma. Shri Krishna did not benefit anything out of Kurukshetra. At the end of the war, in what way was Shri Krishna benefited? He was already a king. He was not bound to help Kauravas or Pandavas. Every person in Kurukshetra was related to him. Loss of a relative in the war would bring great pain and grief to him. Which side should he favour? What he has to consider?

At one instance, Shri Krishna asked Kauravas whether they need his Narayani Sena (army of Shri Krishna) or him alone to be in Kauravas' side during the war. It was an act of balance. He tried to create all amicable situations to dissolve this feud.

However, the biggest question laid down before these manifestations are- how to decide which is right and which is wrong? This is always debatable because of the perception of right and wrong changes from person to person. How we impose our greed and desire, differentiates our way of living. This world runs on a collective bundle of conscious thoughts & actions. Consensus on conscience makes a manifestation to act for a greater good and such deed with self-questioning can discriminate between these two. The outcome of such a selfless deed means a lot to this world. There is no religious identity towards it. There is no dark thought in it.

INTENT MATTERS!!!

The problem here is when things go overboard, everything collapses. For example, any being has an equal right on the source of this Earth. When it goes into hands with an intent to exploit the need and necessity then there is no sustenance in it. There is no act of balance in it. In the same way, when wrongs are not balanced with rights, sustenance will become difficult for the whole gamut. The purpose of existence fails.

Shri Rama always faced a situation where he had to decide between right vs. right. For instance, when Shri Rama had a decision to make about his exile, there were two questions in his mind: As a Kshatriya (not a caste, it is a professional duty) and successor–in-line to the throne, he has to accept kingship (his coronation ceremony was on next day) and as a son to his father, he has to oblige to his father's words. At that juncture, both seemed to be the right path for righteousness. If Shri Rama wanted to become king only for enjoying the sovereignty, he would not have obliged his father's words but he inferred that his kingdom will not go into ruins even if he is not going to take up the kingship. He believed that his brothers are capable of ruling the kingdom selflessly. ***Shri Rama saw sovereignty as a mere duty rather than power.*** As you can see, his idea and action to become a king is for people.

Shri Krishna was very practical. He did what he felt was right and needed at that moment. He knew the fate of Gandhari's curse upon him. Even after taking shame, curse, and grief upon him with self-less intent to establish long-lasting righteousness. Even in the case of Shri Rama, people around inflicted grief upon him, he has to desert his wife to prove his integrity with people of his kingdom. He sacrificed his family life to uphold his duty as a king. Though Shri Krishna and Shri Rama were contrasts in character, the compulsive situations were almost the same. What was common between these two?

1. Both expected no desired outcome or personal benefits for their actions.

2. Both understood the true nature of life. They defined the purpose of living.

3. Both did not run behind their emotions. Their duty did not get maligned by their emotions.

4. In some aspects, they encased their Mind so much that striving for something personal never existed.

These manifestations always acted for the greater good. Though they faced, curse, grief, agony, and inhibitions, their actions never faltered. These manifestations were personifications of realized.

This gamut runs on a collective bundle of different notions on life but all the notions would reach the same destination at some point in time. A juncture where a realized resonates infinity. *A dark yet blissful where sense, sensibility, sensory would make no sense and believing all along becomes non-sense.* A juncture where only Shiva shall encompass.

Understand and unveil SHIVA

Who is Shiva? Or What is Shiva?

We always tend to add attributes to identify an abstract to comprehend in gross form but when we try to personify, we lose the essence of it. The question of who is Shiva? Can be answered by anyone who has read the least amount of scriptures and stories about Shiva's manifestation and his miracles but estranged master differs from it. The whole notion of this scribbling is to make one understand that Shiva is more than the concept of 'GOD', more than the ambit of the creator and created, more than merciful who fulfills the wishes of truthful devotees

And now we shall explore the essence of 'SHIVA'.

Let us forget the attributes of Shiva. Let us ask ourselves, what exactly does Shiva mean?

The reply to this question changes based on the personal beliefs and ideas but as a perpetual truth, 'SHIVA IS BOUNDLESS, SENSELESS AND BLISS"

Can these be considered as attributes of Shiva? The answer is NO and let me explain why?

When you emboss attributes to an abstract, you personify an unknown based on your perceptions without inferring truth. The above said ***are not attributes*** of Shiva.

Being boundless is Shiva, being senseless is Shiva, being blissful is Shiva. What is being Boundless, Senseless and Blissful?

Though humans claim to be independent, in a real sense we are dependent on one and another for living. When a question arises, 'WHAT IF?' this question can alter the complete state of your mind. Though you seem to be peaceful and calm if something is snatched away from you, would you be in the same state of mind?

The independent attitude which we showcase in our life is absolutely fake. It is not about gross needs, it is about a perpetual state of mind where your understanding, needs, existence will not change even if something is snatched from you and when your life becomes a big question.

In reality, humans are real free being but we shackle ourselves voluntarily. The basic needs of a human always change according to circumstances. If you are thrown into a jungle, your whole purpose of living construes down to survival. You tend to eat whatever is available around but when you get so accustomed to your life in Jungle, you tend to get bored and expect something more in your life. The same happens when you are in society. When you are among people, your purpose of living shall be more than just survival. But defining the purpose of living is self– imposed as you tend to give weightage for life as defined by the majority.

What makes you attached to these people around and things around you? Is it a destiny by default? If you eat the same food again and again without some purpose, you tend to get bored and expect something 'better'. There is nothing called satiation in life. If people all around get satisfied without pursuing further, the whole world comes to standstill.

Shiva, on the other hand, has neither needs nor desires. Shiva's hunger is depending upon what he gets to eat. Shiva accepts everything. Shiva is always satisfied without depending on anything and anyone. Shiva is not bound by anything and not obligated to anyone. The real free being without any shackles.

Shiva understood that nothing needs to be known except self. Shiva's wants, questions, originates within and ends within. Shiva understood what is considered to be 'need' during the lifetime is only to satisfy the bodily needs and mind falsely assumes that body and mind are the same. Even hunger, thirst, breath do only replenish the body but do not satisfy the mind or alter the state of existence. If there is no hunger or thirst for any human, only desires will rule the whole world and if there are no desires, the existence of the world becomes questionable. Needs, desires, emotions, actions, reactions provoked by thoughts are the only reasons for this world to be alive, else there is no purpose for this world to exist.

Shiva gazes inwards. Logically, Shiva refrains from seeing anything except Shiva. What connection does Shiva have with this world? Shiva has no obligation, duty or responsibility towards this world. Shiva finds no purpose in seeing the world as it creates only hindrances to reality. Shiva is inert, mere Jada which has infinite energy of the universe imbibed within.

In some sense, Shiva does not come under the definition of living because Shiva is beyond Jiva's sensible comprehension. This is the reason, Jiva is not able to experience Shiva. As discussed before Jiva tries to experience only with sensory and senses but Shiva is supersensuous.

How Jiva, Shava & Shiva are interrelated. Let us try to simplify it:

Jiva – Living, existence

Shava- Dead or gross body without Jiva.

Shiva –Boundless, Senseless and Bliss

As said, Shiva is inert by nature and does not fall under the ambit of existence through senses. Jiva is full of vitality, active and subtly proves its existence by actions, thoughts, reactions backed with consciousness and so on. Shava is a state where prana disappears from the body but consciousness cannot be identified as our understanding of consciousness through actions, reactions, and expression of thoughts disappear. We understand that when prana disappears from body, Jiva becomes Shava but where does this mind go?

Contrary to the end of life, Shava might be a stage of shedding old skin for a new skin. It might be an altered state of existence and not devoid of existence. Maybe, we fail to recognize it. Our senses fail to sense it and our mind has not been trained to realise, as it has been proficiently trained to view life in a particular way where it assumes everything bound with the body is real. We are not trained to disintegrate ourselves to identify reality.

When Jiva becomes Shava, it becomes Shiva by accident. What does this mean?

When Jiva becomes Shava, it is freed from all ties, it has no obligations and no duties towards anything and anyone. It is free from all worries, emotions and portrays only bliss. In simple, when Jiva becomes Shava, it unveils SHIVA by accident and you fail to realize it. Though Jiva becomes boundless and senseless at this juncture, there shall not be any bliss and unless you realize it, you shall be only Shava. From estranged master's metaphysical point of view, this is the reason where ignorance cannot be considered as bliss.

As said, at the juncture of Shava, Jiva unveils Shiva by chance but fails to recognize it because of ignorance. Only during life, Jiva can experience and understand the reality by shutting down hindrances of external factors with the help of mind for realizing boundless, to becomes senseless and radiate bliss by enquiring self and unveiling Shiva.

But one question remains unanswered – How Shiva is related to Jiva? How Shiva is related to this world?

As an essence, Shiva is not related to this world. To simplify further 'The WORLD' which we define. Boundless, Senseless and Bliss makes Shiva a universal truth. The ultimate reality. You cannot tag anything with Shiva, right from the subtlest of energy to grossest form. Shiva can be vaguely compared as an infinite seed of universal consciousness constricted within.

But how Shiva is related to Jiva – The answer is simple

JIVA IS SHIVA WHEN REALISED.

By nature, Jiva is boundless, Senseless and blissful. Voluntary shackles bind Jiva and make him sensible, pragmatic to lead this life as a dutiful and responsible person. When these dutiful, responsible, practical, logical thoughts are followed by conscious actions then inertness gets layered by the functional and lively world. Since you are born, you are bound to your duty and since you are trained to be responsible, dutiful and lively your mind fails to understand the reality of inertness. Realisation of reality is in stillness. Shiva can neither be quantified nor qualified. *When every Jiva is Shiva, all the beings on this earth are the same in different skins.*

By essence, Shiva is unquantifiable. If there is an ever-flowing river which is filled up in different bottles, it does not mean that different bottles represent different rivers. In the same way, Jiva is a manifestation as comparable to water in the bottle from the river, cannot be identified once poured into the river i.e. when Shiva gets unveiled.

What about this Bliss? .Being blissful is the ultimate aim of Jiva. When bliss persists, Jiva needs nothing more. When all desires are satisfied and when there no duties or responsibilities, you tend to become blissful.

In a practical sense, there is no way to satiate all the above said except to contend your mind and encase it from inflictions and emotions.

The irony is, when you try to create bliss it tends to falter. When you realize that bliss is your ultimate truth by nature without artificially creating it, you are blissful. When you are born with responsibilities and duties, subsequently needs and desires shroud you. It is unavoidable. Since the inert Shiva becomes lively Jiva, actions without expectations and reactions with constricting emotions can make your mind unaffected by any inflictions while performing your duties and fulfilling your responsibilities. The key is disintegration and differentiation.

As a spirit, Jiva is Shiva and by virtue, Jiva can unveil Shiva. This is true nature.

When Jiva is Shiva, what is the true purpose of praying? Which entity does it reach to?

There are two things to it. Shiva is immeasurable. Jiva is mere Shiva with ignorance. A real truthful prayer with **powerful intent** invokes the Shiva in you, from everyone and everywhere across. Though intent for prayer can be considered as a desire in some instances if it is justified by conscience and becomes a reason for creating a sense of happiness around, the purpose of living gets defined. This is the essence of Jiva. As said before, Shiva is beyond comprehension and represents everything; unparalleled power beyond our understanding. A truthful prayer with a conscience makes the gross form of Jiva to answer your worldly needs. This can be from self, from others, from anyone and from anywhere.

Enquiring self and experiencing the abstract shall unveil Shiva in you. This is the ***resonance of reality.***

www.ingramcontent.com/pod-product-compliance
Lightning Source LLC
Chambersburg PA
CBHW050023170726
48282CB00025B/526
9789354063992